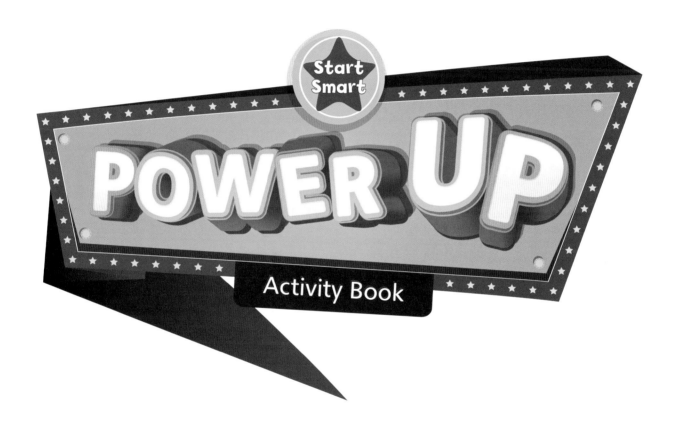

Start Smart

POWER UP

Activity Book

Caroline Nixon & Michael Tomlinson

Map of the book

	Vocabulary	Language	Literature	Phonics and Literacy	Cross-curricular
Hello Page 4	**Main scene vocabulary** *bird, boat, book, bus, cat* **Numbers** *1–6* **Colours** *blue, green, orange, purple, red, yellow*	*Hello. I'm (Jenny/Jim).* *What number's this?* *What colour's this?*			
1 **Friends and family** Page 8	**Friends and family** *man, woman, boy, girl, family* **More family** *mum, dad, brother, sister, pet*	*What's your name?* *My name's … / I'm …* *How old are you? I'm …* *He's/She's …*	***Home time*** A real-life story Skills practice	Initial sounds: introduction	Family trees
2 **At school** Page 18	**School** *bag, classroom, pencil, playground, teacher* **More school** *board, bookcase, chair, cupboard, table*	*What are they? They're …* *Are they … ? Yes. / No.* *Where's my …? Where is it?* *It's in/on/under …*	***The bird and the cat*** A cartoon story Skills practice	Initial letter sound: b	Primary and secondary colours
3 **Food shopping** Page 28	**Food** *apple, banana, grapes, orange, watermelon* **More food** *beans, burger, carrot, egg, rice*	*There's/There are …* *How many … are there?* *A lot.*	***In Mr Brown's garden*** An animal story Skills practice	Initial letter sounds: b, c	Where food comes from
Review Units 1–3					
4 **At home** Page 40	**Home** *bed, clock, computer, lamp, mirror* **Rooms** *bathroom, bedroom, garden, kitchen, living room*	*I've/You've got …* *Have you got … ?* *Yes, I have.* *No, I haven't.* *I/We/They haven't got …*	***The three wishes*** A traditional story Skills practice	Initial letter sound: c	Shapes at home

Hello

1 **Point and say the names.**

Hello. I'm (Jenny/Jim).

1 Draw and say.

1 Draw lines and say.

1   **2**   **3**   **4**   **5**   **6**

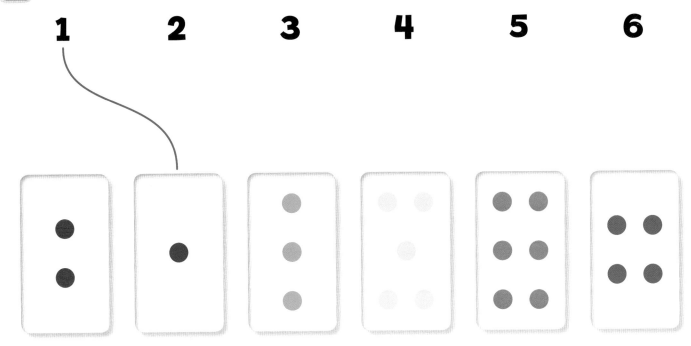

2 0.02 Listen and circle. Say.

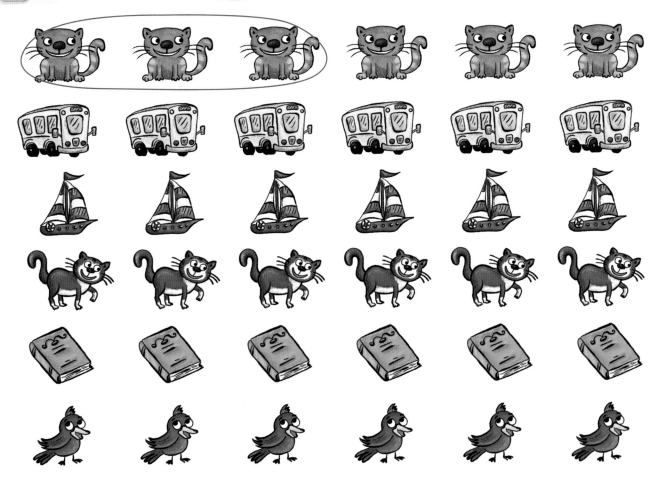

1 🎧 0.03 Listen and (circle) the tick ✓ or cross ✗.

2 🎧 0.04 Listen and colour.

Friends and family

1 🎧 1.01 **Listen and draw lines. Listen again and colour. Say.**

Friends and family *man, woman, boy, girl, family*

1 🎧 1.02 **Listen and number.**

2 🎧 1.03 **Listen and (circle) the tick ✓ or cross ✗.**

1 🎧 1.04 **Listen and number.**

2 🎧 1.05 **Listen and draw lines.**

More family *mum, dad, brother, sister, pet*

1 🎧 1.06 **Listen and circle the tick ✓ or cross ✗.**

2 🎧 1.07 **Listen and colour.**

1 **Point and say.**

2 **Draw Ben and May. Point and say.**

3 **Is home time at your school the same or different?**

Text type: A real-life story

1 🎧 1.08 What's this? Look and say. Listen and check.

1

2

3

4

5

6

2 🎧 1.09 Listen and colour.

1 🎧 1.10 1.11 Listen, point and say the number. Listen and say the words.

2 🎧 1.12 Draw lines. Listen and repeat.

Initial sounds: introduction

1 Look and colour red or blue. Say.

2 Draw your family tree. Talk to a friend.

My family

The Friendly family

1 🎧 1.13 **Listen and (circle). Who is it?**

1

2

3

4

Story: Vocabulary and language in context

1 🎧 1.14 Listen and colour.

2 Self-evaluation. (Circle) Cameron.

At school

1 🎧 2.01 **Listen and colour. Say.**

2 **Look and draw. Point and say.**

1

2

3

4

School *bag, classroom, pencil, playground, teacher*

1 🎧 2.02 Listen and number.

2 🎧 2.03 Listen and circle.

1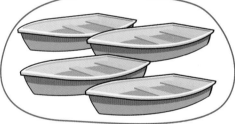

2

3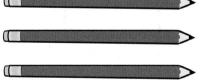

4

What are they? They're ... Are they ...? Yes. / No.

1 🎧 2.04 **Listen and (circle) the tick ✓ or cross X. Say.**

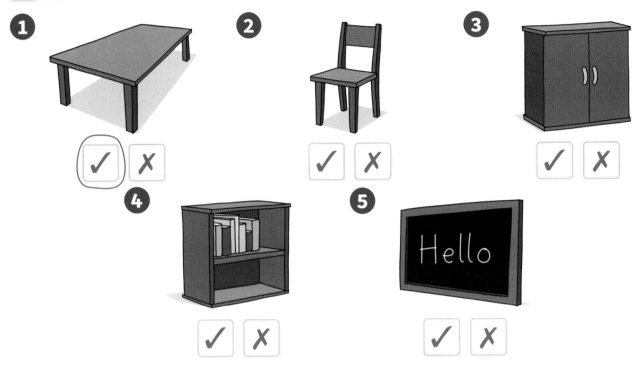

2 🎧 2.05 **Listen and draw lines.**

1 🎧 2.06 Listen and point. Listen again and colour.

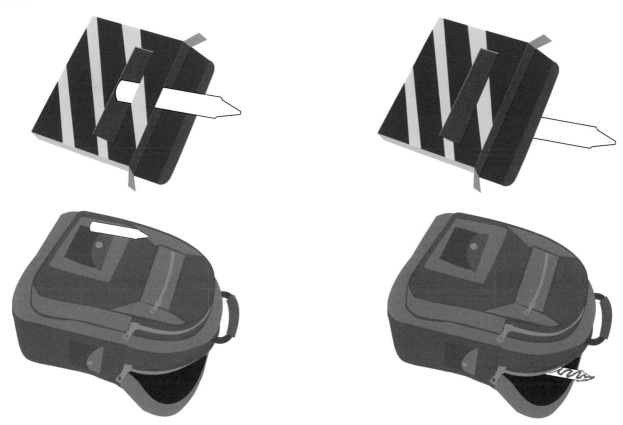

2 🎧 2.07 Listen and draw lines.

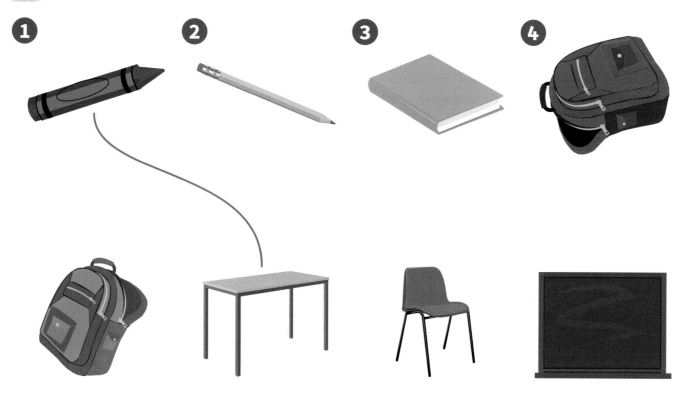

1 **2** **3** **4**

Where's my …? Where is it? It's in/on/under … 21

1 **Number the pictures in order.**

2 🎧 2.08 **Look and listen.** (**Circle**) **the tick ✓ or cross ✗.**

Text type: A cartoon story

3 🎧 2.09 **Listen and colour.**

1 2.10 **Listen and point.**

2 **Cross out X the picture that doesn't start with b. Say.**

1

2

3

4

1 Look and colour. Say.

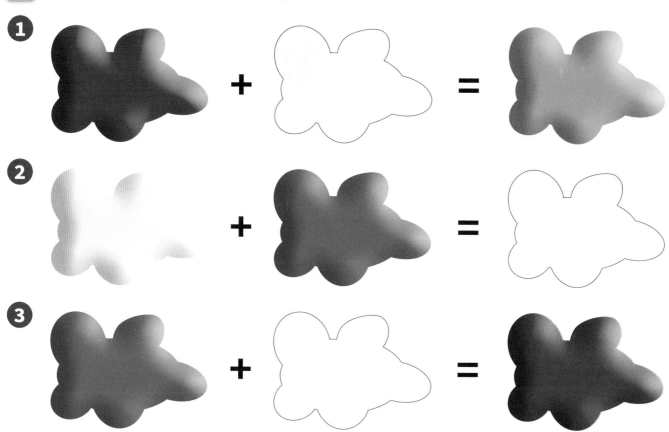

1
2
3

2 (Circle) primary colours in blue and (circle) secondary colours in orange. Ask and answer.

The Friendly family

1 🎧 2.11 Listen and (circle) the tick ✓ or cross ✗.

Story: Vocabulary and language in context

1 🎧 2.12 Listen and colour.

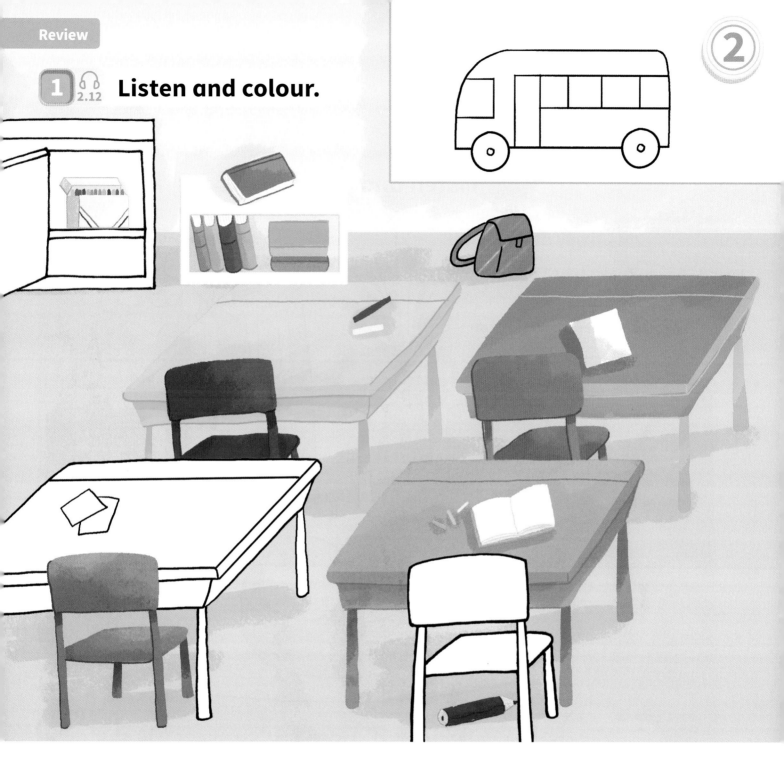

2 Self-evaluation. Circle Cameron.

3 Food shopping

1 🎧 3.01 **Listen and colour. Say.**

2 **Where is the food? Ask and answer.**

Food *apple, banana, grapes, orange, watermelon*

1 🎧 3.02 **Listen and draw.**

2 🎧 3.03 **Listen and colour.**

1 Listen and number.

2 3.05 Listen and draw lines.

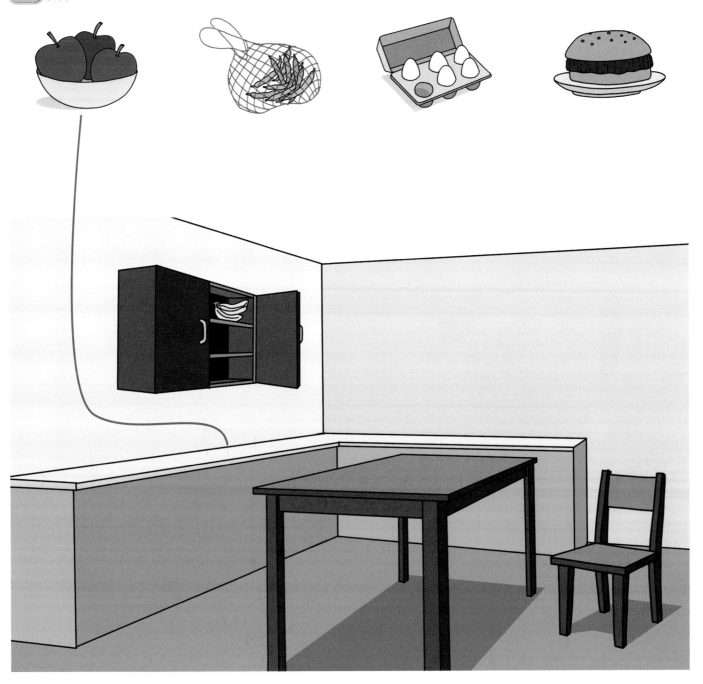

More food *beans, burger, carrot, egg, rice*

1 🎧 3.06 **Look at the pictures. Listen and (circle).**

❶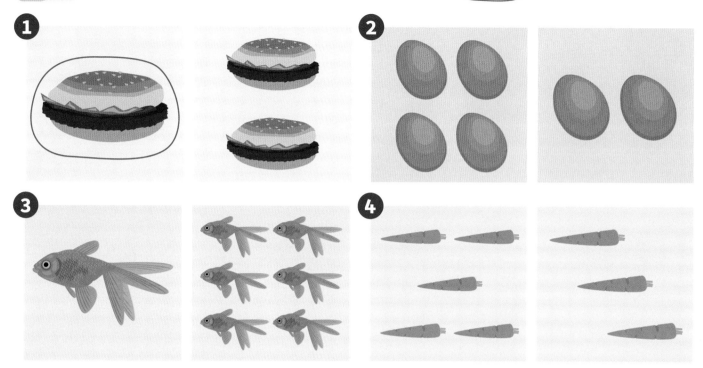

❷

❸

❹

2 **Count and write the number.**
Ask and answer *How many ... are there?*

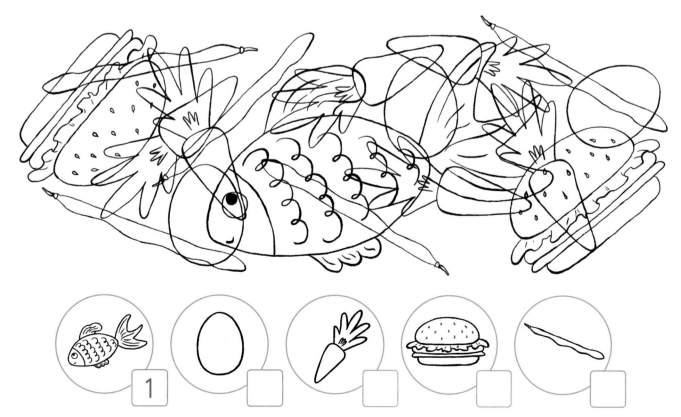

1

1 Number the pictures in order.

2 Tick ✓ the food Rabbit takes.

Text type: An animal story

3 Look at the picture. Answer your teacher's questions.

1 **Write the letter b round the beans and bananas. Colour.**

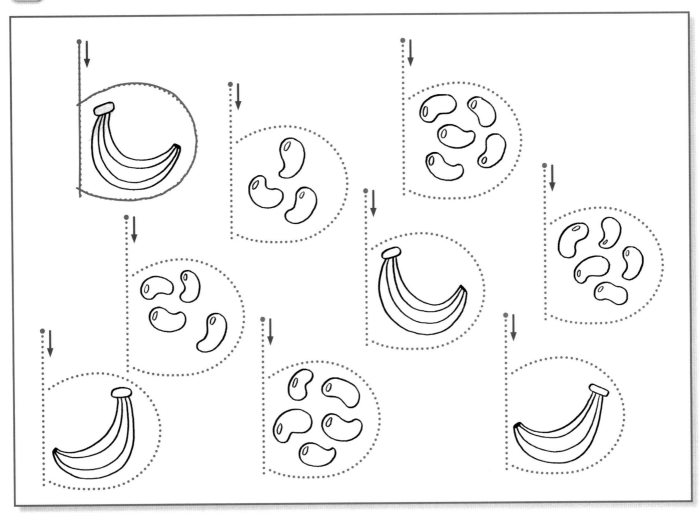

2 **Write the letter c to complete the caterpillar. Colour the caterpillar and the carrot.**

1 **Look and draw lines. Say.**

2 **Draw and colour your food.** (Circle) **in red or yellow.**
Talk to a friend.

1 🎧 3.07 Listen and number.

③

1 🎧 3.08 **Listen. Draw and colour.**

2 **Self-evaluation. Circle Cameron.**

1 🎧 3.09 **Listen and colour.**

2 🎧 3.10 **Look at Activity 1. Listen and ⬭circle⬭ the tick ✓ or cross ✗.**

1 ✓ ⬭✗⬭ **2** ✓ ✗ **3** ✓ ✗

4 ✓ ✗ **5** ✓ ✗ **6** ✓ ✗

3 Choose 6. Tick ✓ and say.

4 Play the game. Say and ⟨circle⟩ your ticks ✓.

At home

1 4.01 Listen and draw lines. Ask and answer.

boat   clock   crayons   computer

lamp

mirror

2 Read and draw lines. Say.

bed   mirror   clock   computer   lamp

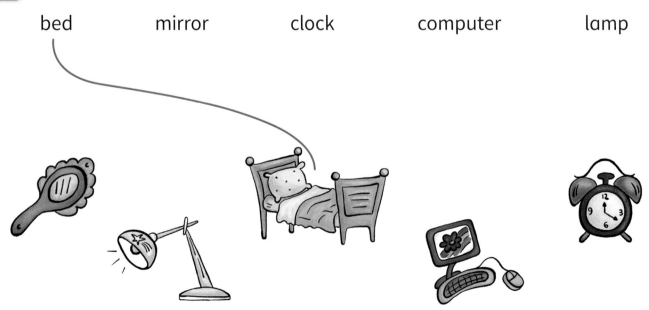

1 🎧 4.02 🎧 4.03 Listen and draw lines. Listen and check.

2 🎧 4.04 Look. Listen and (circle) *yes* or *no*.

1 (yes) no   2 yes no   3 yes no
4 yes no   5 yes no   6 yes no

I've/You've got … Have you got …? Yes, I have. / No, I haven't.   41

1 🎧 4.05 **Listen and number. Say.**

2 🎧 4.06 **Listen and (circle) the rooms the correct colour.**

1 4.07 **Listen and cross out X.**

Lucy

Sam

Kim

2 4.08 **Listen and number. Say.**

1

1 (Circle) the wishes.

2 🎧 4.09 Listen and (circle) the correct word.

1. mirror / (fish)   2. house / classroom   3. house / garden

4. bed / clock   5. book / lamp

1 🎧 4.11 **Listen, point and say. Colour the words that start with c.**

2 🎧 4.12 **Say. Listen and draw lines.**

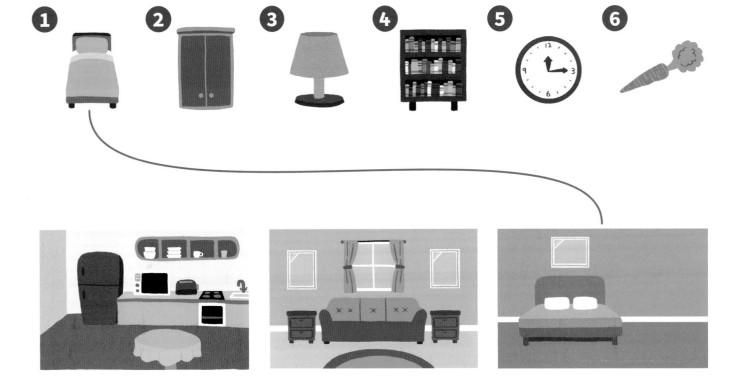

1 **Look and colour. Say.**

1 🎧 4.13 Listen and tick ✓ or cross ✗.

1 ✓

2

3

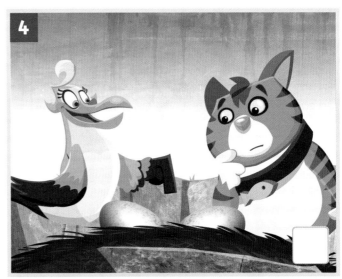

4

5

6

④

1 4.14 **Listen. Draw and colour.**

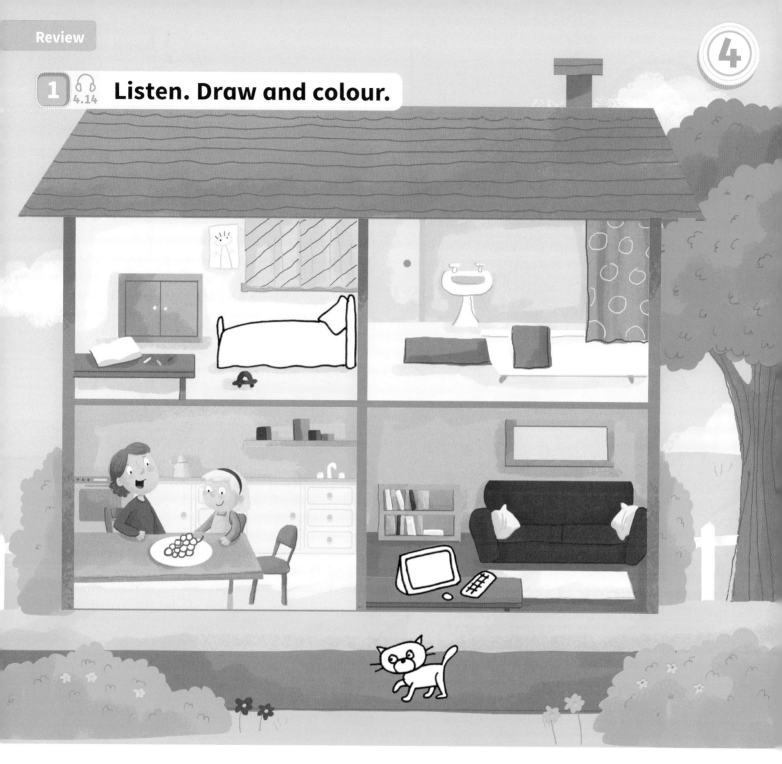

2 Self-evaluation. (Circle) Cameron.

5 My body

1 Write. Draw lines. Colour.

ears   eyes   legs   mouth   hair

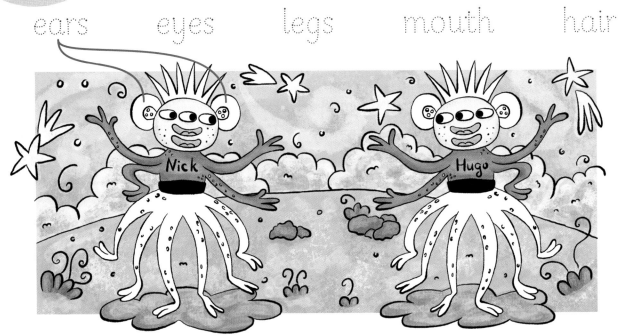

2 🎧 5.01 **Look. Listen and number.**

1 _____ 5 _____

2 _____

3 _____

4 _____

5 _____

6 _____

1 🎧 5.02 Listen and draw lines.
Use red for Pete and blue for Grace.

Pete   Grace

2 🎧 5.03 Look. Listen and write *yes* or *no*.

1	yes / no	2	yes / no	3	yes / no
4	yes / no	5	yes / no	6	yes / no

He's/She's got … Has he/she got …? Yes, he's/she's got …   51

1 🎧 5.04 **Listen and tick ✓ or cross ✗.**

2 🎧 5.05 **Listen and write. Say.**

long / short hair

small / big ears

a short / long leg

a big / small mouth

1 🎧 5.06 Listen and cross out X.

Sam

Dan

2 🎧 5.07 Listen and tick ✓ or cross X.

Alice	X		
Tom			
May			

1 **Look and read.** (Circle) **the correct words.**

1 big / (small) ears

2 red / brown hair

3 brown / blue eyes

4 a big / small mouth

5 long / short hair

6 short / long legs

LUCY

2 **Look at the pictures. Look at the letters. Write the words.**

❶

d o g

❷

____ ____ ____

❸

____ ____ ____ ____

❹

____ ____ ____ ____

❺

____ ____ ____ ____

❻

____ ____ ____ ____

1 🎧 🎧 5.08 5.09 **Cut out the pictures. Listen and say.**
Listen and put the words in the right baskets.

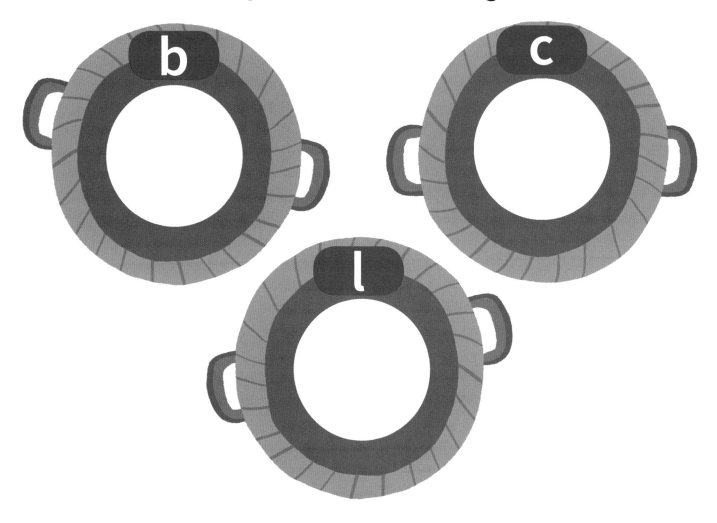

2 **What has got legs? Circle and say.**

1 Look and draw what's missing. Write.

brush my teeth   wash my face   wash my hands

2 Who is keeping clean? Look and tick ✓. Say.

1

2

1

3

4

1 🎧 5.10 Listen and number.

1 🎧 5.11 **Listen. Draw and colour.**

2 **Self-evaluation. Circle Cameron.**

6 My toys

1 Write. Draw lines.

train   teddy   doll   camera   board game

2 6.01 **Listen and draw lines.**

Sue   Alex   Eva   Bill

1 🎧 6.02 Listen and **circle**.

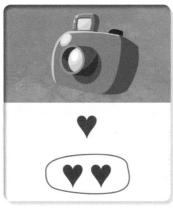

♥

♥ ♥

♥

♥ ♥

♥

♥ ♥

♥

♥ ♥

♥

♥ ♥

♥

♥ ♥

2 🎧 6.03 Listen and draw lines.

Jill and Dan

Hugo and Tom

Grace and Lucy

♥ ♥

♥ ♥

♥

♥

♥

♥ ♥

1 (Circle) and say the word. Write.

1 (ball) / book

2 plane / pencil

3 bike / bird

4 car / cat

5 balloon / banana

2 🎧 6.04 Listen and draw lines.

1 🎧 6.05 Listen and cross out X.

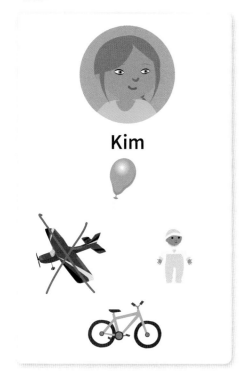

2 What do you like? Look and write *yes* or *no*. Ask a friend.

You

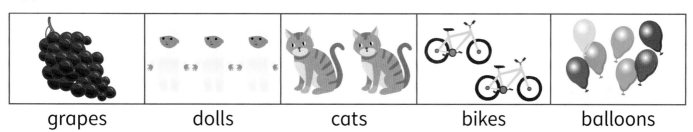

| grapes | dolls | cats | bikes | balloons |

_____   _____   _____   _____   _____

Your friend

| grapes | dolls | cats | bikes | balloons |

_____   _____   _____   _____   _____

1 **What do they give Mandy? Draw the toys.**

2 **Tick ✓ and colour Mandy's favourite toy.**

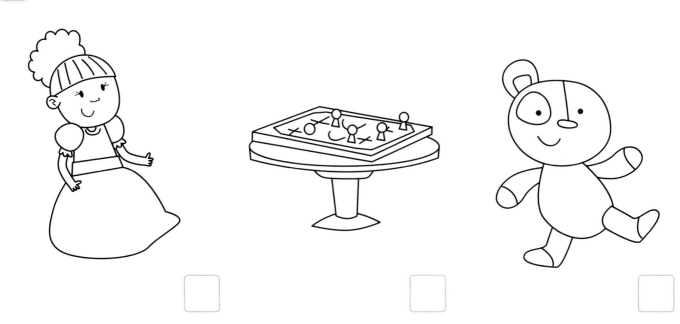

Text type: A real-life story

3 🎧 6.06 **Listen and draw lines.**

Mandy   Freddy   Ann

Ben   Bill   Sue   Jill

1 🎧 6.07 🎧 6.08 Listen and say. Listen and draw lines.

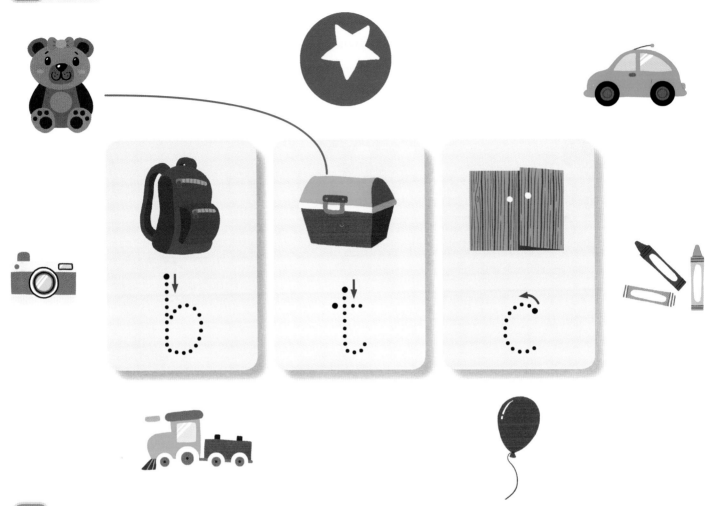

2 Look and say. Write the letter t or l.

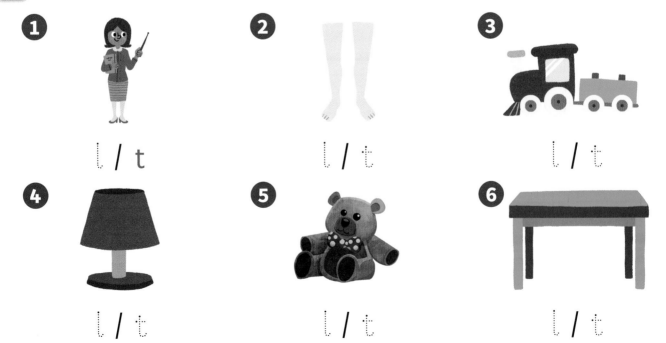

1 l / t

2 l / t

3 l / t

4 l / t

5 l / t

6 l / t

1 **Look and write.**

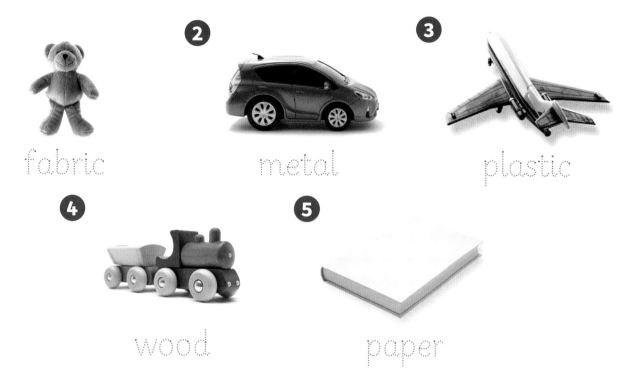

1 fabric

2 metal

3 plastic

4 wood

5 paper

2 **Draw your favourite toy. Write and tell a friend.**

My favourite toy is my _____ . It's made of _____ .

The Friendly family

1 🎧 6.09 Listen and tick ✓ or cross ✗.

Story: Vocabulary and language in context

1 🎧 6.10 Listen. Draw and colour.

2 Self-evaluation. (Circle) Cameron.

1 Draw lines and colour.

= lamp = bed = car

= teddy = ball = computer

2 🎧 6.11 Look. Listen and write *yes* or *no*.

1 _____yes_____ 2 _____ 3 _____

4 _____ 5 _____ 6 _____

3 Choose 6. Write and say.

mirror   mouth   train   garden   doll   bathroom

camera   bike   clock   balloon   legs   kitchen

4 Play the game. Say and (circle) your words.

7 Free time

1 Write.

run / jump   walk / jump   walk / swim

jump / climb   run / swim 1

2 7.01 **Listen and number.**

1 7.02 **Listen and number. Listen again and write *yes* or *no*.**

_____

_____

_____

_____

_____

_____

2 7.03 **Listen and tick ✓ or cross ✗. Write *can* or *can't*.**

1

✗

Mark ____can't____ sing.

2

Mark _____ run.

3

Mark _____ walk.

4

Mark _____ jump.

Can you …? Yes I can. / No, I can't. I can …   73

1 🎧 7.04 **Listen and draw lines. Use the colours you hear. Write.**

~~play~~   fly   play   catch   play

1 Alice

2 Hugo

3 Sam

4 Eva

5 Matt

a ball

play football

basketball

the piano

a plane

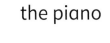 **2** 🎧 7.05 **Listen and tick ✓ or cross ✗.**

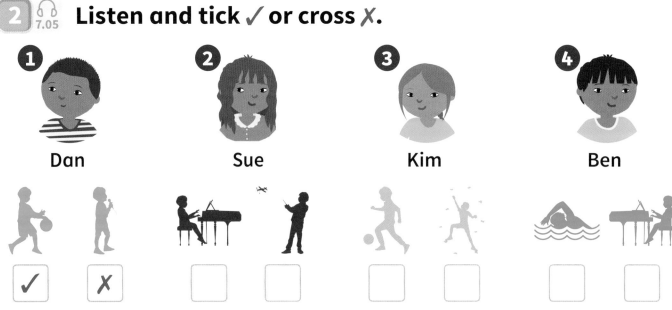

1 Dan

2 Sue

3 Kim

4 Ben

| ✓ | ✗ | | | | | | |

1 🎧 7.06 **Listen and number.**

2 🎧 7.07 **Listen and draw lines.**

1 Alice   **2** Matt   **3** Hugo   **4** Eva

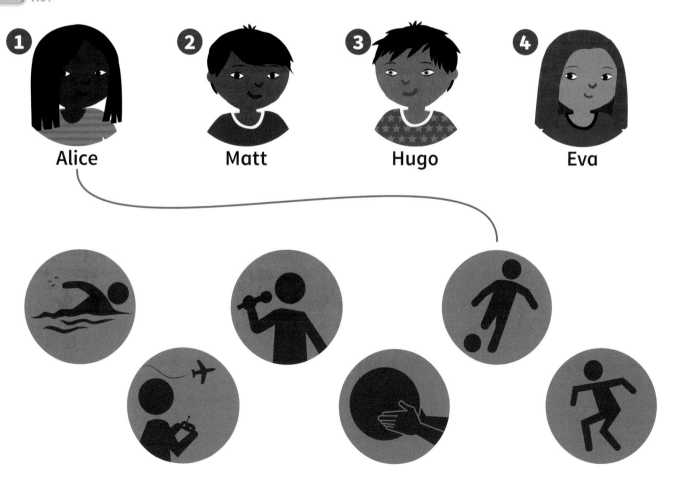

What are you doing? I'm ...ing.

1 Read and (circle) the correct word.

Cat
can / can't climb.

Frog
can / can't swim.

Toad
can / can't sing.

1

Flamingo
can /(can't) swim.

Frog
can / can't jump.

Toad
can / can't jump.

2 🎧 7.08 Listen and number.

3 Draw pictures of something you can do, and something you can't do. Tell a friend.

4 Look and read. Tick ✓ or cross ✗.

1

These are dolls. ✗

2

These are balls. ☐

3

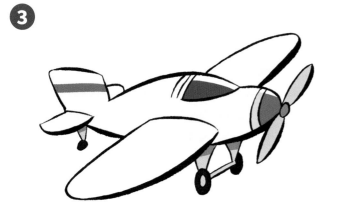

This is a train. ☐

4

This is a cat. ☐

5

These are apples. ☐

6

This is a bird. ☐

1 7.09 7.10 **Listen, point and say. Listen. Draw a circle around the f words and a square around the p words.**

2 **Write the letter f or p.**

1

f

2

3

4

5

1 **Point and say. Write.**

angry ~~happy~~ sad scared tired

1

She can swim.
She's h a p p y .

2

He can't play basketball.
He's _____ .

3

She can't fly a plane.
She's _____ .

4

He can't walk.
He's _____ .

5

She can't jump.
She's _____ .

2 **What emotions do you sometimes feel? Draw you. Write.**

I'm _____ .

I'm _____ .

1 🎧 7.11 Listen and number.

1

Story: Vocabulary and language in context

1 🎧 7.12 Write. Listen. Draw and colour.

~~ball~~ balloon piano plane

b a l l

_____

_____

_____

2 Self-evaluation. Circle Cameron.

8 We're having fun!

1 **Read and ⊙circle⊙ the word.**

1
⊙clean⊙ / eat

2
sleep / clean

3
eat / take a photo

4
clean / drink

5
sleep / eat

6
drink / take a photo

2 **Write and say.**

I'm **p l a y i n g** basketball.

cleaning   drinking   eating
~~playing~~   sleeping   taking

1

2
I'm _____ a burger.

3
I'm _____.

4
I'm _____ a photo.

5
I'm _____.

6
I'm _____.

1 Listen and number.

 1

2 🎧 8.02 Read and ⬭circle⬭. Listen and check.

1

(It's)/ It isn't climbing.

2

They're / They aren't playing basketball.

3

He's / He isn't playing the piano.

4

They're / They aren't swimming.

5

She's / She isn't jumping.

6
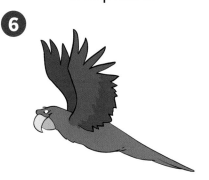
It's / It isn't eating.

I'm …ing.   83

1 **Look and write.**

beach   ~~bird~~   flower   sea   sun   tree

1 b i r d

2 _ _ _ _ _

3 _ _ _ _ _

4 _ _ _ _ _

5 _ _ _ _ _

6 _ _ _ _ _

2 8.03 **Listen and draw lines. Use the colours you hear.**

1 Bill

2 Eva

1 🎧 8.04 Listen and number.

Alex ☐

Pat 1

Sue ☐

Kim and Tom ☐

May ☐

2 Read and write *yes* or *no*.

1 Is Pat taking a photo? _yes_
2 Is Sue jumping in the sea? ____
3 Are Kim and Tom playing basketball? ____
4 Is Alex sleeping? ____
5 Are the birds catching fish? ____
6 Is May eating watermelon? ____

What's he/she …ing? What are you/they …ing? He's/She's …ing. They're …ing. 85

1 **Tick ✓ the actions from the story.**

2 **Look at the pictures in Activity 1. Circle the actions.**

w	s	c	l	e	a	n	k	n	e
e	t	d	p	a	m	i	u	g	d
s	m	h	a	t	o	s	f	w	r
w	a	l	k	a	n	t	l	g	i
i	l	y	s	n	a	y	y	e	n
m	u	j	k	f	m	o	e	a	k
m	s	l	e	e	p	i	s	g	i
t	a	k	e	a	p	h	o	t	o

clean
drink
eat
fly
sleep
swim
take a photo
walk

Text type: A fantasy story

3 🎧 8.05 **Listen and tick ✓.**

1 What are Bird Boy and Dog Girl having for lunch?

2 Which is Bird Boy's favourite photo?

3 Where is Dog Girl's phone?

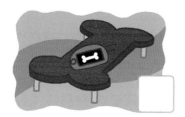  

4 Who is Bird Boy talking to on his computer?

5 What are Cat Boy and Dog Girl doing in the garden?

 **1** 8.06 8.07 **Cut out the pictures. Listen and say. Put the words in the right baskets. Listen and check.**

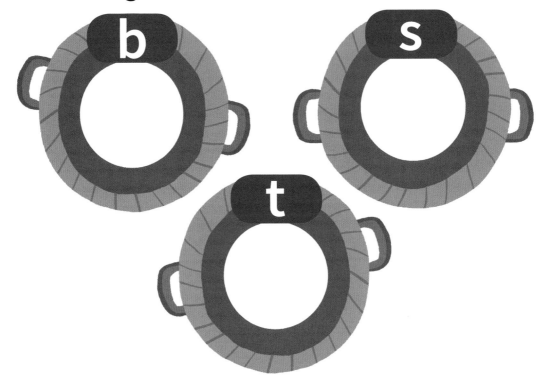

2 8.08 8.09 **Listen, point and say. Draw a (circle) around the b words, a square around the s words and a triangle around the t words. Listen and check.**

⑧

1 **Look and draw lines.**

It's windy.   It's sunny.   It's cloudy.   It's snowy.   It's rainy.

2 **Draw you in your favourite weather.**
What are you doing? Write.

It's _____.   I'm _____.

The Friendly family

1 🎧 8.10 **Listen and number.**

Story: Vocabulary and language in context

1 🎧 8.11 **Write. Listen. Draw and colour.**

balloon̶ bike camera sun

b a l l o o n

2 **Self-evaluation. (Circle) Cameron.**

Moving to the farm

1 **Read and match. Colour.**

1	2	3	4	5
			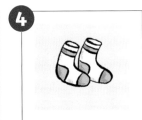	

shoes   T-shirt   socks   jeans   jacket

2 **Write.**   jacket   jeans   shoes   socks   ~~T-shirt~~

1  It's a ___T-shirt___ .

2 They're _____ .

3 It's a _____ .

4 They're _____ .

5 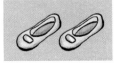 They're _____ .

1 🎧 9.01 **Listen and draw lines. Use the colours you hear.**

1  Sue   **2**  Eva   **3**  Lucy   **4**  Dan

2 **What do you want? Choose 4. Circle and write.**

      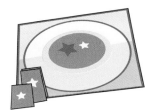   

teddy   bike   board game   camera

computer   doll   piano   ball

1   I want a _____ .   2   I want a _____ .

3   I want a _____ .   4   I want a _____ .

1 Write. cat dog duck goat horse sheep

1

cat

2

3

4

5

6

2 🎧 9.02 **Listen and circle .**

1

2

3

4

5

1 🎧 9.03 Listen and number.

1

2 🎧 9.04 Write. Listen and check.

clean   climb   ~~play~~   take

1 Let's _play_ basketball.

2 Let's _____ the shoes.

3 Let's _____ the tree.

4 Let's _____ a photo of the horse.

Let's … Yes, OK/great/please. / No, thank you.

1 **Number the pictures in order.**

2 **Draw your favourite animal from the story. Who is it? Write the word.**

I like _____ the best.

3 **Look and read. Write *yes* or *no*.**

Examples

There's an apple tree.	yes
The dog is running.	no

Questions

1 The man's T-shirt is blue. _____
2 There are five animals. _____
3 The duck is swimming. _____
4 The horse is small. _____
5 The horse is eating a carrot. _____

1 🎧🎧 9.05 9.06 **Listen, point and say. Listen and play Bingo!**

2 🎧 9.07 **Listen, point and say. Write the letters b, c, f, l and s to make the words.**

C at   b us   ___ag   ___ish

___ed   ___amp   ___eg   ___un   ___ock

1 **Look and write what animals need.**

food   shelter   water

1

2

3

Animals need _____ .   Animals need _____ .   Animals need _____ .

2 **Draw you looking after an animal. Write.**

My animal is a _____ . It needs _____ .

The Friendly family

1 🎧 9.08 Listen and tick ✓ or cross ✗.

1 ✓

2

3

4

5

6

Story: Vocabulary and language in context

Review

1 9.09 🎧 **Write. Listen. Draw and colour.**

horse   jacket   jeans   ~~shoes~~

s h o e s

2 **Self-evaluation. ⟨Circle⟩ Cameron.**

1 🎧 9.10 (Circle) the word. Listen and number.

running /
(jumping)

swimming /
drinking

flying /
swimming

catching /
walking

singing /
cleaning

sleeping /
running

2 Do you want these things? Choose four and tick ✓.
Write. Ask a friend.

	Me	My friend
some flowers		
a jacket		
a horse		
a piano		
a T-shirt		
🐕 a dog		

I want

_____.

I want

_____.

I want

_____.

I want

_____.

3 **Choose 6. Write and say.**

duck   T-shirt   flower   shoes   tree   goat

jacket   beach   sheep   socks   sun   jeans

4 **Play the game. Say and (circle) your words.**

Thanks and Acknowledgements

We would like to thank all of the people involved in this project. In particular, we wish to thank Maibritt Shah and Jane Holt for their hard work, enthusiasm and attention to detail, and Kimberly Russell for her editing. As always, we are enormously grateful to Liane Grainger for her vision and unflagging good humour.

Dedications

For my parents, Pauline and Eric Nixon for allowing me 'supported self-determination' during my formative years. – CN

For Javier, María José and Laura. It's a privilege to have you as friends. – MT

The authors and publishers acknowledge the following sources of copyright material and are grateful for the permissions granted. While every effort has been made, it has not always been possible to identify the sources of all the material used, or to trace all copyright holders. If any omissions are brought to our notice, we will be happy to include the appropriate acknowledgements on reprinting and in the next update to the digital edition, as applicable.

Key: U = Unit.

All the photos are sourced from Getty Images.

U1: JGI/Jamie Grill; Ariel Skelley/DigitalVision; MoMo Productions/DigitalVision; incomible/iStock/Getty Images Plus; RDC_design/iStock/Getty Images Plus; **U3:** Bruno Scramgnon Chagas/EyeEm; Arisara Tongdonnoi/EyeEm; Roland Magnusson/EyeEm; Sarote Impheng/EyeEm; Anthony Lee/OJO Images; Mint Images/Mint Images RF; Vicki Smith/Moment; Gisela Rentsch; KeithBishop/DigitalVision Vectors; VICTOR-/DigitalVision Vectors; **U5:** Jose Luis Pelaez Inc/DigitalVision; Klaus Vedfelt/DigitalVision; Dean Mitchell/E+; Michael H/DigitalVision; GrashAlex/iStock/Getty Images Plus; Siqui Sanchez/Moment; Catherine Delahaye/DigitalVision; **U6:** Suchart Doyemah/EyeEm; Taya Gokita/EyeEm; CSA Images; JoKMedia/E+; studiocasper/E+; **U7:** Alistair Berg/DigitalVision; NickS/E+; hanapon1002/iStock/Getty Images Plus; Image Source/Photodisc; mediaphotos/E+; Rafa Elias/Moment; Anna Pekunova/EyeEm; JGI/Jamie Grill/Tetra images; Highwaystarz-Photography/iStock/Getty Images Plus; BananaStock; **U8:** AlinaMD/iStock/Getty Images Plus; mammuth/E+; Pobytov/E+; Jon Paul Perry arranginglight.com/Moment; Enrico Ladusch/EyeEm; **U9:** Banar Fil Ardhi/EyeEm; Stephanie Starr/EyeEm; bluecinema/E+.

Illustrations: Antonio Cuesta; Beth Hughes; Arnold From The Big Red Illustration Agency; Cesar Samaniego; Dan Crisp; Dean Gray; Gaby Zermeno; Genie Espinosa; Hannah Wood; Iryna Boiko; Jake McDonald; James Hearne; Kelly Kennedy; Lesley Danson; Marek Jagucki; Tony Trimmer.

Cover page illustrations and photography: Tony Trimmer; leremy/iStock/Getty Images Plus/Getty Images; PrettyVectors/iStock/Getty Images Plus/Getty Images; bennyb/iStock/Getty Images Plus/Getty Images; NatuskaDPI/iStock/Getty Images Plus/Getty Images; Yevhenii Dubinko/iStock/Getty Images Plus/Getty Images; Vectorpower/iStock/Getty Images Plus/Getty Images; MaryMo_art/iStock/Getty Images Plus/Getty Images; ComicSans/iStock/Getty Images Plus/Getty Images; StudioM1/iStock/Getty Images Plus/Getty Images; Tatiana Zhzhenova/iStock/Getty Images Plus/Getty Images.

Cover design and illustrations: Blooberry Design

Audio recording: Ian Harker

Additional writers: Angela Llanas, Lucy Frino , Bill Parminter, Julieta Hernandez Rodriguez, Karen Elliot, Garan Holcombe

Freelance editing: Lauren Cubbage, Steph Howard

Song and chant composition: Robert Lee

Song and chant audio production: Ian Harker and Jake Carter

Video production: Phaebus Media Group

Animation production: Q2A Media Sevices Pvt. Ltd.

Production project management: Mónica Palacios, Shirish Mishra

Additional editorial project management: Pablo Fernandez de Cordoba

Design lead: Hannah Todd

Asset manager: Gemma Wilkins

Permissions controller: Ajay Yadav